TROUT
FISHING
MADE EASY

Published by Hyndman Publishing, PO Box 5017, Dunedin
ISBN 1-877168-91-2 • TEXT: © Mike Weddell • DESIGN & ARTWORK: Dileva Design Ltd
• PRINTING: Spectrum Print

2

TROUT
FISHING
MADE EASY

Trout Fishing Made Easy

Introduction

Trout fishing in its many different forms is often portrayed as a difficult 'art' but nothing could be further from the truth. Trout fishing is as simple or as complicated as you wish to make it. Having the right tackle, setting it up correctly and using it logically can enable you to enjoy some success right from the start. It doesn't matter whether you spin, bait fish or fly fish; approaching fishing in a careful, systematic manner is the way to go.

We are lucky here in New Zealand where world class trout fishing is available to all at a relatively modest cost so make the most of it.

The following pages will help you to get started, or if you have already started, help increase your enjoyment and catch rate.

Trout – All You Need To Know

To be a successful angler you need to realise that it is the fish that call the shots – so it helps to be aware of some of the shots they will call. The better our understanding of trout the more likely we will be to catch them.

Trout, rather like humans, want to eat as much as possible without expending much energy and this fact alone dictates their feeding habits.

Being territorial, trout usually live in particular parts of rivers or lakes for a long time. Brown trout will inhabit a specific location for years, while rainbows may remain in an area for a season. If the trout are to stay there, the territory must have certain characteristics. Well oxygenated water is most important; in addition there must be a good food supply, suitable feeding places, and safe areas to shelter in when threatened.

In running water good feeding places occur where the current carries a supply of food past a place where a trout can lie sheltered from the current. The fish swims out into the current to take the food before moving back into slack water. In stillwaters trout have to swim to find food so generally have a usual route which they patrol. Food in stillwaters is most concentrated near weedbeds or the mouths of streams.

In streams fish take refuge under boulders or undercut banks, beneath trees or in deep water. In stillwaters they shelter in weedbeds and deep water.

Straight away these facts highlight ideal places to seek trout, such as on the edges of ripples in streams and around stillwater weedbeds. All the same, it is one thing to know where to look for trout, and quite another to be successful at catching them. Trout, being wild, have instincts which enable them to survive. We can outwit them more easily by being aware of their defences.

7

Vision

Trout have good eyesight; they have colour vision and can see quite fine detail. It is important for us to know about their field of vision. In their normal swimming position, trout cannot see directly below them, and will take items of food that are level with, or above them, in the water. So, the bait or the lure must be at the correct depth if a trout is to see it.

Trout do feed off the bottom, particularly in stillwaters, and swim in the distinctive position of tail up and nose down, so they can see the bottom close before them.

Their vision is binocular immediately in front of them and monocular on either side. They can see to the rear but have a small blind spot behind and below – approaching a trout from behind avoids spooking it.

The trout's eye differs from the human eye, as its pupil cannot dilate or contract according to the amount of available light. As a result, trout

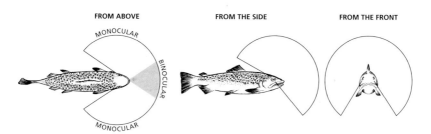

FROM ABOVE   FROM THE SIDE   FROM THE FRONT

are somewhat dazzled in bright sunlight, and often easy to approach. However they see very well in overcast weather, when they can be very difficult to catch.

Trouts' eyes are well adapted to feeding in the dark. They can see things close to and above them, but very little that is further away. Consequently night fishing, especially fly fishing is an effective way to catch trout, but try to master your technique in daylight first.

Trout can detect movement easily; if you can see a trout assume that it can see you, so move slowly if you have to move at all. It is easier for trout to see you if you are on the skyline, so keep away from it. Cover is useful when approaching trout – cover behind you is just as effective as cover in front. While you can still be seen, cover behind makes you much less obvious, while cover in front can hide you altogether.

Hearing

Children who go fishing with adults are often told to keep quiet in case they scare the fish; so they believe that trout can hear human voices. If trout can hear human voices it doesn't seem to concern them too much, but other sounds can alarm them. Sound is the result of air vibrating – trout 'hearing' detects vibrations in the water. Heavy footfalls on the bank, gravel crunching or rocks knocking together can be detected. The background noise of ripples appears to mask other sounds, so trout cannot detect sounds close to ripples as well as they can in flat water.

Feeding

Trout feed whenever the opportunity arises - if something edible comes along they will eat it. They tend to concentrate on one type of food if it is abundant, sometimes to the exclusion of everything else.

As we have already explained, trout need to feed efficiently, avoiding swimming against the current, but staying close enough to benefit from the food it carries. The size of the food item is relevant because a trout will swim some distance for a large item such as a small fish or a cicada but not for a midge or willow grub. Similarly in stillwaters a trout will go further from its usual route for a large item of food than a small one.

Trout Food

Trout wherever they are found, have adapted to a habitat which provides cool, well oxygenated water. This also applies to the creatures that trout feed on, so no matter where trout are found, their diet is fairly similar. However, the major factor that dictates their diet is whether they live in flowing waters or stillwaters. A lesser factor governing the variety of food available is the creatures that may be blown onto the water from the surrounding countryside.

Insects play a large part in the diet of trout and these are best imitated by fly fishing although some such as cicadas and grasshoppers and beetles can be fished with bait fishing tackle.

Trout also feed on worms and grubs and these make excellent baits in all waters and any state of water.

In some waters and at certain times of year small fish play a large part in the diet of trout. Trout feeding on these can be caught with naturals or spinning baits.

9

RAINBOW TROUT

BROWN TROUT

SEARUN BROWN TROUT • RESIDENT BROWN TROUT

BROOK TROUT

Spinning and Bait Fishing Tackle

Having the right tools for the job always makes life easier and this is especially true of spin fishing, and luckily the same tackle can be used effectively for bait fishing. Never buy tackle just because it is cheap, buy it because it will do the job; if it is cheap that is a bonus.

In this chapter we will look at tackle for spinning and bait fishing and how to set it up to get the best from it.

Rods

The size and strength of a rod is governed by where we wish to fish and the size of the fish likely to be caught. Many spin fishers under-rod themselves and many bait fishers are guilty of the complete opposite using tackle that is far too heavy. Selecting a rod and a matching reel and line of medium weight and power enables both forms of fishing to be carried out effectively.

A rod in the length range of 2metres to 2.15metres is a good starting point and it should be capable of casting a weight of between 5gm to 15gm. The actual weight of the rod is not critical but the lighter the better especially if you are casting continuously for long periods. Carbon fibre is the ideal material although it is more expensive, but good fibreglass rods are not far behind performance-wise and can be quite a bit cheaper.

Actions of rods vary a lot from sloppy to very stiff; somewhere in the middle is about right. How can you tell? Wiggle the rod and if it flexes right down to the handle it is too sloppy and if it hardly flexes at all it is too stiff. Ideally try casting with a rod before you buy it. With a 10gm weight it should flex but not buckle.

The spacing and number of the guides is important. If there are too few guides and the spacing is too wide near the top, the rod will not

13

cast well and will flex too much at the tip. A good quality rod of the recommended length will have at least 6 guides including the tip. The butt guide should be at least 25mm. Guides that have a ceramic lining will last a lot longer than plain metal guides but are more expensive.

Good quality rods will usually have a cork handle. Cork feels better when it is cold and wet, but if everything else is right don't let the absence of a cork handle put you off.

The fitting that holds the reel can be simply two sliding rings or a screw fitting. The sliding rings are lighter but less secure, but don't buy a rod with a very heavy screw fitting - the lighter the better.

It is a good idea to wax the joint where the two sections of your rod meet as this prevents them becoming loose and the top flying off when casting and it reduces wear of the joint.

The rod should be given a rub down with a soft damp cloth occasionally.

It is a good idea to keep your rod in a tube when not using it or carrying it to or from fishing, reducing the chance of damaging it. You can make one from plastic drainpipe or buy one ready made.

Reels

A good reel is more important than a good rod when it comes to spinning. Most spinning in New Zealand is done with threadline reels as these are the easiest to learn to use. We are lucky today as spinning reels are light years ahead of those made only 20 years ago. Buy the best you can afford. A good reel will last for years; a cheap one won't last long and worse, it may give up the ghost while you are out fishing.

Don't buy a reel that is too big. It should be big enough to hold 150-200metres of the line suitable for the type of fishing you do. There is no point in using a reel that will hold hundreds of metres of line that you will never use. A big reel will be heavier than a smaller one and ideally

the whole outfit, rod, reel and line should be as light as possible.

Features that are desirable in a reel are instant anti-reverse, a T shaped rubber handle, a titanium ball bearing bale and a titanium lip on the spool. A spare spool is always worth having to carry a spare line, but don't leave it at home. It should always be carried on the water, just in case.

Ideally the forefinger of the rod hand should be able to touch the lip of the spool while gripping the rod normally. This enables the line to be controlled when casting as we will see later.

Reels need more looking after than rods and should be kept clean and lubricated. Oil, however, should be used sparingly as it shouldn't ooze out and get on the line. If the reel grates, as it will when it gets dirt behind the spool, remove the spool immediately and rinse in water.

Line

Again, modern lines are a great improvement over their predecessors, much thinner and more durable for a given breaking strain. Most trout fishing can be done successfully with a line breaking strain between 2.5 and 4kg although there are a few occasions where something heavier may be called for. The line, more so than reel or rod, determines how far a lure of a given weight can be cast. The lighter the line the further you can cast.

There is a choice between nylon monofilament lines and braided lines. The former is recommended for beginners as it is easier to control and a lot cheaper.

Buy a monofilament for its breaking strain and ideally it should have good knot strength and be resistant to abrasion. Line should be checked regularly for abrasion. If any roughness is found cut the line at the reel side of the abrasion and retie your tackle as when the strain comes on, the line will break at any abrasion.

So that great lengths of line are not lost when breaking on a snag it is worthwhile fishing with a short length of thinner line next to the lure or hook so that is all that is lost when a break occurs.

It is important to have the right amount of line on your reel. If the reel is overloaded you will get frequent tangles when casting and if the reel is underloaded casting distance is reduced.

Hooks

The simple rule with hooks is to use the best you can get and don't use hooks that are too big, especially when bait fishing. Depending on the size of fish you expect to catch and the size of your bait, hooks should generally be in the range #12 to #6.

There is much controversy about single and treble hooks when spinning. I don't think it matters much as long as you obey the local regulations.

So far we have covered the essential items of tackle. The business end, lures, swivels and weights will be covered later but there are other items which, while not essential, make life a lot easier.

Tackle Boxes

Small partitioned plastic boxes are useful for carrying lures, hooks, weights and swivels.

This helps keep them in order and easily located when you need them. Boxes with ventilation holes are preferable as this allows items to dry out after use and helps stop rusting.

Polarising Glasses

These glasses allow you to see into the water not only to spot fish but to better assess the depth of the water. They also protect your eyes from the

glare from the water on a bright day. Wrap round models are the best. Pale lenses are preferable as you can still use them in low light conditions.

Landing Net

Using a landing net is the quickest and easiest way to land trout. It is possible to beach fish but steep banks often prevent this. A net is essential in a boat. There are all shapes and sizes but remember if you are not fishing from a boat it needs to be carried around and if it is too big it can be a nuisance.

Tackle Bag or Fishing Vest

Either of these items is useful for carrying all your tackle on the water. Vests are usually associated with fly fishing but are just as useful for other forms of fishing. Whichever you choose it needs to be able to hold tackle, lunch and of course fish.

18

Line Cutter

This could be nail snips, scissors, or knife or angler's line snips - it doesn't matter which as long as they are sharp. Line snips on a retractable reel are probably the most convenient.

This list is far from exhaustive but should allow you to fish successfully. Clothing and waders are down to personal preference.

Knots

Using the correct knot and tying it properly goes a long way towards preventing tackle failure. Knots are the weak links in any tackle set up and care needs to be taken when tying them to reduce the chance of failure.

There are dozens of knots used by anglers but there are certain criteria that a knot must meet to make it useful. It should be quick and easy to tie and weaken the line as little as possible.

Blood Knot

One knot pretty well fits the bill for attaching lures, hooks, flies and swivels and it is variously called blood knot, clinch knot or barrel knot. To make it as strong as possible it must be tied correctly. The diagram shows how to tie it but it needs to have 6 to 8 turns and should be pulled up from the reel end first, then from the line end and then the reel end again. It should also be pulled up slowly until it is firm; don't try to break it.

BLOOD KNOT

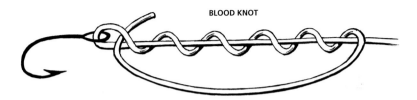

19

Surgeon's Knot

This is a quick, simple, easy-to-tie knot that is strong and reliable and is used for joining two pieces of nylon such as tippet to fly leader. It is important to pull the knot up evenly on all four ends for the strongest possible result. Three turns are needed for fine tippets but for thicker nylon two will suffice.

SURGEON'S KNOT

LEADER

TIPPET

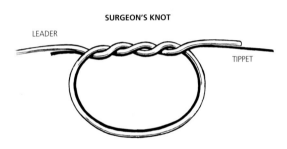

Casting

Many spin fishers and baitfishers never learn to cast properly; they do themselves a great disservice. Being able to cast accurately is a great asset not only in catching fish but in not losing lures, hooks and sinkers. Knowing the correct techniques combined with a little practice pays dividends over and over again.

For accuracy over a short distance underhand casting is the best. For accuracy over a greater distance a straight overhead cast is best, while an around-the-side cast gives maximum distance.

The Grip

Casting for trout is a single handed business. Hold the rod with your preferred casting hand with the stem of the reel between your second and third fingers and hook the line with the tip of your forefinger pressing it against the rod handle. All the other hand has to do is click the bail arm back so that the line will run free when you cast.

Underhand Cast

To cast underhand let your lure hang about 60cm below the tip ring, lift your hand a little to raise the rod tip and the lure will begin to swing. As it swings back towards the rod, raise the tip quickly with a flick of the wrist and at the same time push your hand forward. At the end of the wrist flick, release the line from the forefinger and the lure will fly away from you close to the water. Too late a release and the lure will go up in the air without going forward, too early a release and the lure will drop well short of the target.

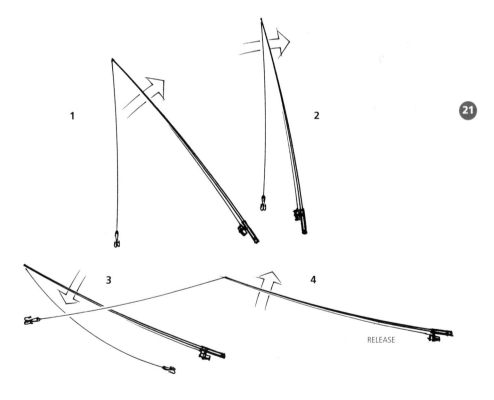

RELEASE

UNDERHAND CAST

Overhead Cast

To make the overhead cast have about 75cm of line between the tip ring and lure, lift the rod hand up and at the same time tip the wrist back so that the rod and lure go back over the shoulder. When the lure has swung backwards as far as it is going to go, bring the hand down at the same time as flicking the wrist. Again as soon as the flick is completed release the line from the forefinger. It takes a little practice to get the trajectory right. Too early a release and the lure will fly high and too late it will nose-dive onto the water close in front.

OVERHEAD CAST – Back cast

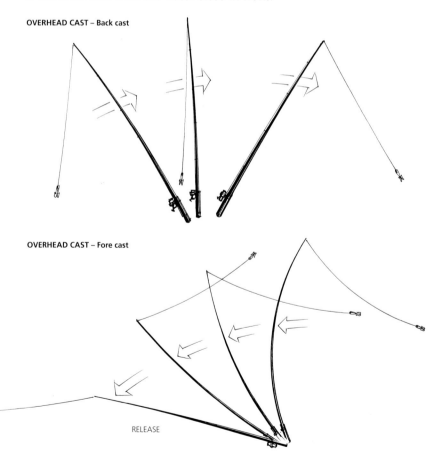

OVERHEAD CAST – Fore cast

RELEASE

Side Cast

With about 75cm of line out from the tip ring start with the rod pointing straight in front. Sweep it quickly round to the right (for a right handed caster) until it is past the midline of the body. A brief pause allows the lure to continue swinging back. Before the lure begins to drop bring the rod forward in the same plane and once the rod comes to the midline of the body, give a vigorous flick of the wrist and release. Point the rod along the line as the lure flies through the air. Try to cast at an elevation of about 45 degrees for maximum distance. If you release too early the lure will fly off to the right and too late it will swing around to the left.

As soon as the lure hits the water turn the reel handle to engage the bail arm and begin the retrieve. Occasionally you may wish to fish deep; then let the lure sink for a while on slack line before engaging the bail arm.

When bait fishing, unless you are using very tough bait, it pays to cast smoothly and with less force so that the bait is not flicked off. Whatever happens, maintain a tight line to lure or bait whilst casting. There should be no slack until the final release.

23

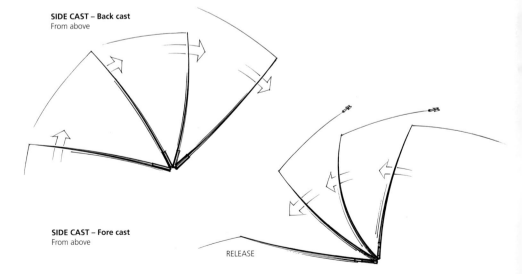

SIDE CAST – Back cast
From above

SIDE CAST – Fore cast
From above

RELEASE

Tackling Up

Spinning

When you have loaded the line onto your reel it is a good idea to keep a swivel tied to the end of the line. This makes the end easier to find when it comes to tackling up. Use a swivel that is appropriate to the thickness of your line. The wire of the swivel eye should be slightly thicker than your line. If the wire is too thin it will cut your line and if too thick will not turn or cast well. Assemble your rod after waxing the joint then attach the reel, lining it up with the guides. Thread the swivel and line through the guides then tie about 50cm of a slightly weaker line to the other end of the swivel. Then tie your lure to the end of this lighter trace.

The next step is to set the reel drag so that a fish that is hooked will not break the line. If the drag is too tight breaks will occur; if it is too slack it will be hard to hook fish and impossible to wind them in. To set the drag, hook the lure onto a fence or branch close to the ground and have about 3metres of line between the rod tip and the lure. Lift the rod until it has an even bend in it. Then adjust the drag so that any extra lifting of the rod makes the drag slip. This drag should be roughly right for fishing – any minor adjustments can be made as you fish.

It is worth remembering that if the lure gets snagged or you are playing a fish, do not continue to wind in with the reel if the drag is slipping as every turn of the handle puts 3 twists into the line and very quickly the line will begin to kink up and will tangle on casting.

If your line does get kinked cut off the lure, trace and swivel then pull out 30 or 40metres of line and walk round a grassy paddock for a few minutes trailing the line behind and the kinks will disappear. Then retie the trace and lure.

Some lures spin in the water and often a swivel is not enough to stop the line kinking. In this situation an anti-kink vane should be attached to the swivel at the top of the trace.

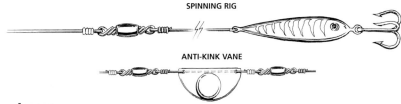

SPINNING RIG

ANTI-KINK VANE

Lures

There are literally thousands of lures available to spin fishers and there will be certain lures that are favoured on your local waters. You should have a few of those but much of the time the choice of lure is not critical unless trout are feeding on a specific food. If trout are feeding on smelt for instance, it makes sense to use a lure that imitates smelt in size, shape and colour.

A common mistake is to use a lure that is too big in clear water and often a dull lure works better in clear water especially if it is sunny. Equally a large bright lure is often more effective in coloured water. A black lure can also do well in coloured water. So it pays to have a range of lures in different sizes, weights and colours.

25

On the Water

Rivers and Streams

There are two main approaches to spinning on a river or stream. The first is to cover all the water systematically, casting down and across to the far bank and retrieving as the lure swings in the current. Repeat a couple of times then take a step downstream and cast again. This way most fish nearby should get a look at your lure and give a chance of catching something.

The speed of the lure is governed by the rate that you turn the handle of the reel and it is a good idea to vary the speed. It is also important to remember that small fish can only swim so fast and if you retrieve too fast especially if you are pulling your lure against a strong current, it will not look natural to the trout.

Casting downstream is not the only option. You can work in the opposite direction, working your way upstream covering all the water by casting upstream at an angle. However the retrieve must be fast enough to keep the lure from snagging on the riverbed.

Exploring the water systematically will catch plenty of fish in waters where there are plenty to catch, but in waters less well populated with trout or small streams it pays to be more selective where you cast. As you gain experience you will begin to identify areas that are more likely to hold trout, such as behind boulders, in channels between weedbeds or beneath overhanging bushes. Target these areas and this is the time that accurate casting pays off.

One mistake that beginners especially often make is to stand casting in one place over and over again. Trout in rivers tend to hold station and if you do not get a take after two or three casts, either any trout there do not like your lure or there are no trout there so keep moving. There is an exception to this rule when trout are running up rivers to spawn, either trout coming into estuaries from the sea or running into lake tributaries. You will find there are certain positions where running trout stop to rest before moving on. If you know of such a spot it is worth sticking to.

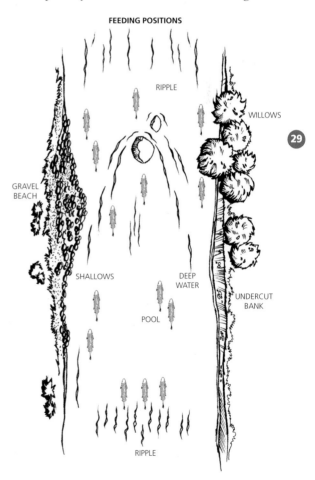

FEEDING POSITIONS

RIPPLE

WILLOWS

29

GRAVEL BEACH

SHALLOWS

DEEP WATER

UNDERCUT BANK

POOL

RIPPLE

Stillwaters

From the angler's and the trout's points of view the main difference between flowing water and still water is that trout have to move around to find food as there is no current to bring it to them. This means that an angler can stand in one spot and expect to have trout moving past at least some of the time, but of course some spots are better than others.

Trout will tend to congregate where there is a more plentiful supply of food such as where a tributary runs into the lake or where a river runs out. Weedbeds too harbour trout food. Brown trout in particular inhabit the shallows of a lake and they can be found in water just a few centimetres deep. Spinning in such shallow water can be difficult but one way of overcoming bottom snags is to use a floating lure with slow retrieve so that it just dips under the water. Another area that is worth a try is on the drop off from shallows to the depths.

Windy days are usually better than calm days with the spinner and since trout tend to feed upwind it is a good idea to fish from a shore parallel to the wind as trout will be moving through the area you are fishing into.

Fishing around river and stream mouths in the autumn and winter when trout are waiting to run up to spawn can be very productive. Browns spawn in May and June but rainbows in prime condition at this time of year follow them to feed on their eggs. Target the rainbows as the browns are not worth catching and should be returned if caught. Rainbows spawn in the spring and should be avoided then but at this time browns come into their own.

It is important to find the depth at which trout are feeding in stillwaters as your lure needs to be near them to stand any chance of making a catch. If you are not catching fish vary the depth of your lure. To increase the fishing depth, give it longer to sink before commencing the retrieve. The retrieve needs to be slower too, to keep the lure deep; too fast a retrieve will pull it back towards the surface.

Trolling

When trolling from a boat, depth is critical. Depth can be adjusted by the speed of the boat, the length of line that is out and the weight of the lure. There is also a gadget called a down rigger that allows you to fish at an exact depth and can be very effective used in conjunction with a fish finder.

Your lure should appear to act naturally especially in terms of speed and this means your boat should be moving slowly. The depth can then be adjusted by lengthening or shortening the line. At least 50 metres of line out would be a starting point.

Real bait fish would not swim in a straight line indefinitely so it pays to change the direction of the boat regularly, fishing in a zig-zag rather than a straight line.

Brown trout will usually be caught in relatively shallow water and rainbows in deeper water or at the drop off, where the slope of the bed suddenly steepens.

Remember the speed of the boat when trolling should be slow – small fish that your lure is imitating can only swim slowly. Try and imagine a small fish swimming and set your speed at that level. Trolling back and forward across river mouths can be effective when fish are waiting to run the river.

31

Bait Fishing

Bait fishing is much maligned but it can be a very skillful and productive method of fishing. There are many and varied ways of presenting your bait to trout whatever that bait may be. But the two most effective positions for the bait are close to the surface or on the bottom. There are various configurations of tackle which enable the bait to be presented where you want it.

Bottom Fishing

A weight is usually used to take the bait to the bottom and hold it there until a trout comes along. It is a common mistake to use too much weight. Some anglers' tackle would be more at home surfcasting off a beach. Use as light a weight as you can get away with. It should be just heavy enough to cast and hold the bottom and no more. This weight can be fixed to the line or can slide along the line but should be just heavy enough to hold it in the current. If the current is very strong it would probably be more effective to allow the bait to drift downstream than to try and hold it still; this way there is a better chance of getting the bait near a trout as more water is covered. Holding the bait on the bottom is more suitable in eddies or slow pools where trout are moving about when feeding.

A rig that works well for bottom fishing is to have a weight with a hole through it above the swivel at the top of the trace. The hook at the end of the trace is baited up and cast out and allowed to sink to the bottom. This rig allows the line to run through the weight when a fish picks up the bait. The bail arm should be disengaged so that when a fish moves off with the bait the line is free to run out and it will feel no resistance. When the fish stops running is the time to strike and set the hook. To stop the line running out while waiting for the fish to bite hold the rod with the line held in the crook of the forefinger. As soon as a bite is felt let go the line. When the line stops going out engage the bail arm and strike.

Fishing on the bottom is much the same whether fishing flowing water or stillwater as the bait is static in both cases.

A variation on bottom fishing is to fish a bait with a very light weight attached so that the bait can drift around a little. This is a good method on small streams trundling the worm down a ripple into a deep pool. It is also a very good method when a river is high and discoloured. Look for eddies close to the bank and drift a worm through or just let it swirl around in the current. Such eddies can often produce fish after fish as they move into the side to avoid the strong current.

BAIT RIG

| LINE | WEIGHT | SWIVEL | TRACE | HOOK |

Float Fishing

To fish a bait near the surface a float can be used. The most readily available and the easiest to use is a bubble float. The bubble float is attached to the end of the line and from the other side of the float a short trace is attached to carry the hook. The length of the trace determines how high or low in the water the bait is fished. Water can be let into the bubble to increase its weight so that even the lightest baits can be cast out. This way floating baits can be cast easily, for instance a dead cicada can be put on the hook and cast to fish that are taking the naturals from the surface. To make life easier an artificial cicada can be tied on instead of a natural.

A float is useful for running a bait down a stream and helps avoid hooking the riverbed. Cast it upstream and wind in as the float bobs back down the current towards you. It is possible to let it drift on past and on downstream by disengaging the bail arm and letting the line pull from the reel. If a fish takes the bait the float will pull under; then is the time to lift the rod to set the hook. Of course if the bait is being allowed to drift in the current below make sure the bail arm is engaged first.

When fishing with a float in a lake the bait is static unless there is a wind blowing and then the float will drift and it is similar to fishing the current in a river.

The Floating Worm

The commonly called floating worm method does not use a float but just a worm and as small a weight as is needed to cast, usually just a couple of split shot. A spinning tackle or fly tackle can be used. The longer fly rod is better to control the drift of the bait which is cast upstream so that it drifts back towards you. When using fly tackle the cast should be made with a rolling action as a fly cast would flick off the worm. The technique is very like fly fishing with a nymph and is equally deadly.

Baits

When most anglers think of bait fishing they tend to think of worms and worms make very good bait for trout. If you go worm fishing it is a good idea to take a good supply of worms with you as you don't want to spend good fishing time hunting for them. The quickest and easiest way to get worms is to go out on the lawn on a warm damp night and with the aid of a torch pick up worms that have left their holes to move about on the grass. You need to sneak up on them as any vibration will send them scurrying back into their holes. On a good night you can get half a bucketful in no time.

It is also worthwhile toughening them up for a few days by keeping them in a container with torn up newspaper in it. The paper should be torn up into pieces about the size of your hand then crumpled up, dampen it a little then throw in the worms. They will keep a long time like this and will toughen up making them stay on the hook longer.

If you have no worms don't go digging up farmers' paddocks or river banks as there are lots of other baits available. The easiest to find are cased caddis under stones on the bed of the river. These caterpillar-like creatures live in tubes made of sand or small stones. Carefully pull a couple out and put them on the hook. The best way to fish them is to use a light weight and drift them through ripples.

Small fish such as cock-a-bullies and smelt make very good baits and help target bigger trout. They can be fished static on the bottom as with a worm or can be fished sink and draw. This method can be a deadly fishing for sighted trout. The best way to fish them is to thread them onto the line sliding them head first down onto the hook which has some lead wire wrapped around its shank. Hold them in position by half hitching the line around the tail (illust). Cast out into a pool or

BAIT FISH SET-UP

LOOP TO LOOP JOIN

REEL LINE   TRACE

ripple, let the bait sink then lift the rod to draw the bait to the surface, then let it sink again and so on. Trout hit hard on a bait fished like this. Fishing with the bail arm disengaged is best so that when the trout hits you can let the line go. The trout will run then stop. When it stops, tighten up and there is usually a well hooked fish on the end.

A smelt fished in an estuary when seatrout are running can give great sport. Smelt or whitebait will leap out of the water when being chased by trout. When you see this happening cast your smelt among them and fish it sink and draw.

Porina grubs and grass grubs are also good baits as are wasp grubs, the larvae from a wasps' nest, if you can get them without being stung. These baits can all be fished in clear or coloured water, on the bottom or with a float, in stillwater or running water.

37

DARNING NEEDLE EYE CUT TO TAKE TRACE LOOP WHICH IS THEN
THREADED THROUGH THE BAIT FISH FROM MOUTH TO VENT

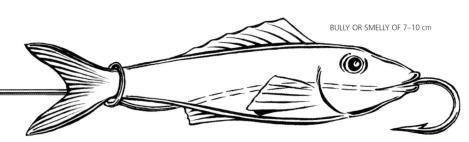

BULLY OR SMELLY OF 7–10 cm

HALF HITCH

Fly Fishing – An Introduction

This section of the book will introduce you to the pleasure of fly fishing, and hopefully remove some of the mystery that surrounds it.

The intention is to equip you with a basic knowledge of tackle, rod and reel, of casting and techniques, that will make your fly fishing an enjoyable experience. A better understanding of these elements brings the likelihood of more success.

The following pages show that fly fishing does not need to be complicated or confusing – some basic knowledge and equipment can give you a start in an activity that can become engrossing and rewarding.

Later you may want to read more. My book "Fly Fishing Made Easy" will supplement the information given here, and will extend your knowledge further.

Tackle and Knots

The range and variety of tackle available can present you with some daunting choices – or just lead to confusion for the novice fly fisherman. You'll obviously need several key items of equipment: a rod and reel, line, leader and fly.

The size of the fly determines the thickness of the leader, which determines the weight of the line used, and consequently the strength of the rod. While owning a range of rods would be the ideal, most of us are more likely to buy one rod to use for all our fly fishing. So our choice of rod will be dictated by the size of the fly we will use most frequently, and the selection of an appropriate reel, line and leader will follow.

The Rod

A good way to get started is to find a fly set which comprises a matched rod, reel and line, usually with a leader and a few local flies included. Most tackle shops stock these. You may want to consider more sophisticated tackle after you gain more experience and skill, but keep in mind that a skilled fisherman using inexpensive equipment will probably achieve better results than an unskilled fisherman with expensive gear – it's the skill that counts.

A rod taking an 8, 9 or 10 weight line is best suited to fishing with feathered lures tied on size 8 hooks or larger. A rod of 5, 6 or 7 weight will be a better choice if you will be using flies from size 10 to 16. The heavier combination is a better choice if baitfish is the main trout food in the waters you fish. Lighter equipment is more suitable if the fish tend to feed more on insects.

For good maintenance of your rod, rub the joints with wax to decrease wear and help prevent the section throwing off when casting. Keep your rod in a carrying case when not in use.

The Reel

41

Fly reels are simple pieces of equipment – they need to hold the fly line and enough backing to suit the kind of fishing you are doing. You need a reel strong enough to stand up to constant use, but still be as lightweight

as possible. Make sure there are no large gaps between the drum and the frame where the line can jam. The more simple the mechanism, the less there is to go wrong. While many modern reels have disc drags (at more expense), even hard running trout can be handled with a simple check mechanism. You can apply extra pressure by pressing your finger on the rim of the reel.

A narrow, large diameter reel will help you recover your line more rapidly than a wide, small diameter model, because the large diameter will retrieve more line per turn of the handle.

If you maintain your reel by keeping it clean and lightly oiled it should have a long life, even with constant use. It's a good idea not to opt for the cheapest model available, and to select one for which you can get spare spools. This means you can carry an alternative line without having to buy a separate reel.

42

The Line

As with other pieces of tackle, there is a huge and often confusing variety of lines available – different tapers, densities, and colours in a multitude of combinations.

Your choice of line will be determined by the type of fishing that you want to do. A floating line is essential for fishing a fly close to, or on the surface. If you want to get the fly down to a certain depth, often near the bottom, you will need a sinking line. The depth of the water and strength of the current will dictate the rate of sink. So to get close to the bottom of deep water with a fast current, a faster sink line will be needed than for shallower or slower water where a lighter density is suitable.

As a beginner and for versatility, choose a floater. By adjusting the length of the leader and weight of the fly, flies can be fished on the surface, just below it, or well below it. This will be your preferred type of line unless you are usually using large feathered lures.

Line Colour

There are varying opinions about the importance of line colour. Some believe that fish are alarmed by brightly coloured lines, but as they see the line from beneath, they can only see a silhouette against the light. Preferably only a small part of the leader tippet should get near the fish, rather than the line passing right over it. It is definitely easier to fish with a coloured line, because it helps us to see what the line is doing and observing the tip of the line tells us when a fish has taken the fly. I used a bright orange line throughout my most successful season.

The Leader

The nylon leader is the tapered link between the line and the fly (or flies). The thin end of the leader to which the fly is attached is called the tippet. Its total length should be about 3 metres, and it can be part of a continuous leader, or added according to the thickness you require. A good strategy is to buy a leader with the heaviest tippet you are likely to need. If you want a finer tippet, knot on a short piece of nylon to suit. The larger and heavier the fly, the thicker the tippet should be.

Frequent tangles in your leader could be caused either by too long a leader, or by poor casting technique, so if shortening your leader doesn't get the right result, it's time to practise your casting.

In windy conditions it pays to reduce the length of your leader. You can do this by shortening the tippet.

Tippet Material

It's useful to carry spools of spare tippet material, in varying diameters and breaking strains, in case you need a finer tippet. When you change flies the tippet gets shorter and will eventually need replacing.

43

Needle Knot

You probably won't need to tie this knot often, and rarely on the riverbank. Tied properly, the leader should stay attached to the line until you think a new one is needed. Keeping the turns in place between finger and thumb as the knot is tightened will give a tidy finish.

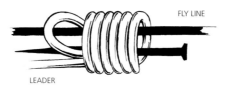

Surgeon's Knot – Refer page 19

Blood Knot – Refer page 19

Try to practise the knots you will need until you can tie them quickly and effectively. This will be an advantage if you need to tie them under pressure on the water, especially if it is cold and windy, the light is poor and the trout are rising all around.

Casting

Casting is a vital aspect of fly fishing. Some will say you don't need to be a good caster to catch fish. While there may be some truth in this, clearly you need to be able to cast well if you want to be good enough to catch fish in most places and under conditions that are less than ideal. If you can't put a fly where you want it most of the time, what is the point of buying good tackle, being an expert at tying on flies and fishing in some of the best waters in the world? You can't just blame the wind, the long grass or the high banks for casts that go wrong, and trout won't take pity on your poor casting and leap at the line, so practise until you can cast proficiently in most conditions.

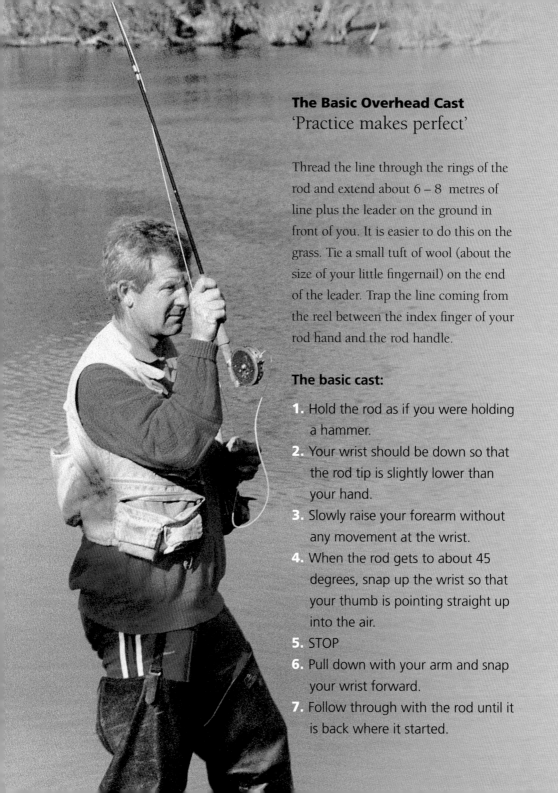

The Basic Overhead Cast
'Practice makes perfect'

Thread the line through the rings of the rod and extend about 6 – 8 metres of line plus the leader on the ground in front of you. It is easier to do this on the grass. Tie a small tuft of wool (about the size of your little fingernail) on the end of the leader. Trap the line coming from the reel between the index finger of your rod hand and the rod handle.

The basic cast:

1. Hold the rod as if you were holding a hammer.
2. Your wrist should be down so that the rod tip is slightly lower than your hand.
3. Slowly raise your forearm without any movement at the wrist.
4. When the rod gets to about 45 degrees, snap up the wrist so that your thumb is pointing straight up into the air.
5. STOP
6. Pull down with your arm and snap your wrist forward.
7. Follow through with the rod until it is back where it started.

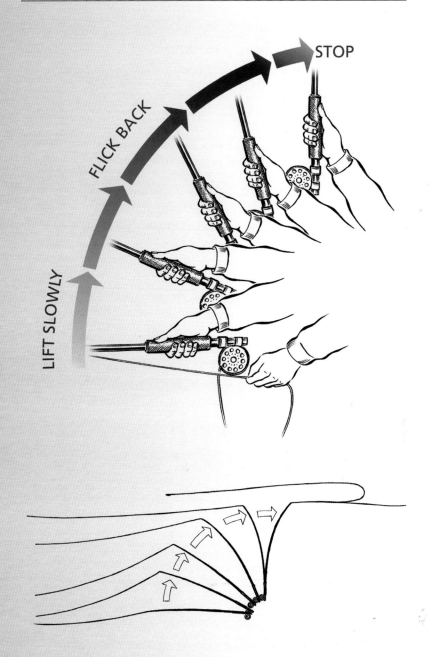

LIFT SLOWLY

FLICK BACK

STOP

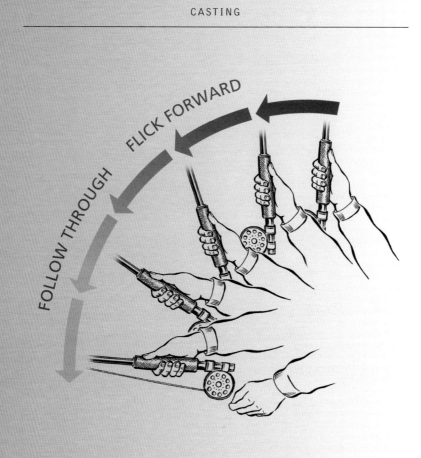

FLICK FORWARD

FOLLOW THROUGH

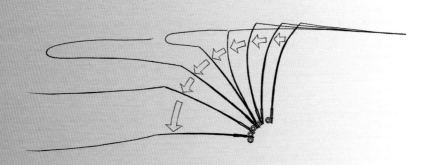

There are some common mistakes to avoid. Make sure your arm starts the casting movement – don't just cast with the wrist. During the cast your hand should move from waist level to face level and back again. Most of your effort is on the back cast – it's easier to think of it as an up cast rather than a back cast. Don't push forward on the forward cast as this stops the line straightening. If the line goes up in the air in front and then dribbles in coils onto the grass, you have taken the rod too far on the back cast.

Make one cast at a time when practising, rather than running one cast into another. Pausing between casts gives you time to make sure the rod is in the correct position to start the next cast. If the line doesn't extend properly, you'll need to change something in your technique to improve this. Practising for no longer than 10 minutes at a time will help maintain your concentration.

Use of the Line Hand

The hand holding the rod controls the cast, and the other controls the line – this is equally as important. It controls the shoot and retrieve of the line and can also pull on the line to increase its speed. In the basic cast where you are just lifting off and recasting a fixed length of line, the line hand does very little. Hold the line between forefinger and thumb with a loop of slack line between the reel and line hand. This stops the line hand resisting the movement of the rod hand during the cast. You should hold your line hand still with the elbow slightly bent throughout the cast. The line hand should not follow the rod hand.

The False Cast

This means casting the line back and forward in the air without letting it touch the water. The first stage, getting the line off the water and into the air, is the same as the basic cast. But next, on the forward part, the arm's downward movement is eliminated. Immediately after the STOP (see page 46) snap the wrist forward without a follow through. As soon as the line has extended forward in the air snap the wrist back again to cast the line to the rear. (See illustration.) This can be kept up until you decide to put the line back on the water. However, try to keep false casts to a minimum – if anything is likely to go wrong, it usually happens while false casting.

Reasons for using the false cast. First, the line can be extended in the air by shooting a little line on each cast. Casting back and forward can also rid a dry fly of water so that it will float when dropped onto the water again. Most fly fishers make too many false casts – 3 should be the maximum. Remember you can't catch fish when the fly is in the air.

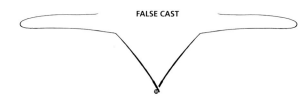

FALSE CAST

Shooting Line

This is a way of extending the line without using false casts to attain distance. Pull a length of slack line from the reel so it hangs between the reel and where it is held by the line hand.

Firstly make your basic overhead cast. When the rod is horizontal, your line hand should release hold of the line – the momentum of the line extended beyond the rod tip will pull the loose line out through the rings.

Releasing your line hand too early results in the line piling up on the water, so release too late rather than too early. The correct timing of the release is immediately after the wrist snap of your rod hand on the forward cast.

At first practise shooting one to two metres of line. While you should be able to shoot over ten metres with more practice, distance is not the primary goal – a short well controlled cast is better than a long messy one, and most fish are probably caught within the 10 metre range on all but the biggest of waters. However, it can be an advantage to be able to make long casts even if you never have to. If you can cast 20 metres, fishing at 10–12 metres will seem easy and you are much less likely to make mistakes.

Fishing to your maximum range all the time causes trouble: you will have more hook ups on the bank behind, more tangled leaders and more splashy casts that scare the fish. You will waste good fishing time removing tangles and retrieving flies from the vegetation on the bank – so always fish at a comfortable distance.

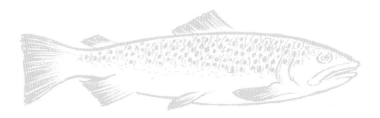

Getting Started

Getting started with a cast is a common problem for beginners – in other words, how do you get enough line out to make the rod work? Thread the line and leader through the rod rings; rather than using the thin end of the leader, it is easier to double over part of the fly line. Tie on the fly, then flick the length of leader and line beyond the rod tip onto the water.

Keep your rod tip close to the water and pull about a metre of line from the reel. Keeping the tip low, move the rod sharply to one side. This will pull the line out through the rings. Repeat several times until there is enough line out to cast. On flowing water the current will carry the line downstream and straighten it; on stillwater the wind may help the line drift out. If it is calm, walk a few paces along the bank, letting the slack line pull out as you go.

Retrieving the Line

You retrieve line to make another cast, to keep contact with the fly when it is drifting, or to move it through the water in a particular way. The first main way to retrieve the line is to pull it in and gather it in loops in the line hand, or drop it to the ground. This allows a fast retrieve. Or secondly, you can gather it in coils in the line hand, but this can only be done slowly. The first method allows the fly to be retrieved in short bursts, while the second allows a more continuous retrieve.

The Strike

While "strike" implies a strong movement, it is better to think of it as tightening onto the fish. Raise the rod till the butt is vertical and you feel the weight of the fish. Avoid any sharp movement or jerking action which could result in a break off, especially if you are using a light tippet.

Playing the Fish

Here, the rules are simple: maintain steady pressure on the fish by keeping the rod up (somewhere between 45 and 90 degrees) and don't let the line go slack. If you have slack line between your hand and the reel, let it out if the fish runs away from you, or pull it in by hand if it runs towards you. This is just as easy as playing the fish from the reel. Remember not to take too long to play out a fish. It should seldom take more than 5 minutes to land even quite a large fish.

Netting a fish is usually the quickest way to get it out of the water. The best way to do this is to place the net in the water, draw the fish over it then lift the net. The fish will be spooked by the net moving about in the water, so keep it still. Hold the fish in the net to remove the hook. It is easier to get the hook out if you hold the trout so it is lying on its back and will not kick.

Choosing the Right Fly

Here is a selection of flies to get you started followed by the lifecycle and description of the trout food they are imitating.

SAMPLE FLY SELECTION

SEDGE PUPA   WOOLLY CADDIS   HARE'S EAR NYMPH

ADAMS   COCH-Y-BONDHU   GREY GHOST

DEER HAIR SEDGE   MRS SIMPSON   JACK'S SPRAT

WATERBOATMAN   BLACK & PEACOCK   MIDGE PUPA

DAMSEL FLY NYMPH   DAMSEL FLY   BLOODWORM

VARIOUS STAGES OF THE INSECT'S LIFE CYCLE

Natural	mayfly nymph	dun	spinner
Imitation	**hare's ear**	**adams**	**adams**
Natural	cased caddis	sedge pupa	adult sedge
Imitation	**woolly caddis**	**bead head hare's ear**	**deer hair sedge**
Natural	brown beetle	green beetle	
Imitation	**coch-y-bondhu**	**coch-y-bondhu**	
Natural	Bully	whitebait	smelt
Imitation	**Mrs Simpson**	**Jack's sprat**	**grey ghost**
Natural	waterboatman		
Imitation	**corixa**		
Natural	bloodworm	midge pupa	adult midge
Imitation	**bloodworm**	**midge pupa/buzzer**	**adams**
Natural	damsel nymph	damselfly	
Imitation	**marabou damsel**	**damselfly**	
Natural	snail		
Imitation	**black and peacock**		

Where these insects can be found.

 = **Streams & Rivers**    = **Stillwaters**

Sedges

SEDGE

ADULT

PUPA

LARVAE

Sedges are related to moths and look very similar when flying. However, sedges are an aquatic insect and both the larval and pupal stages live in the water. There are cased larvae, sandy cased, horn cased and many others, as well as caseless larvae. Both the cased and caseless larvae are taken by trout; so too are the pupae and adults.

Larvae tend to live on the river bed on rocks and stones. They occasionally drift in the current, which is when trout feed on them.

The pupa swims towards the surface of the water where it hatches into an adult. The hatch usually occurs around dusk and on into darkness. Once hatched the adults run across the water to the riverbank and then fly off into the surrounding vegetation. Again during the hours of dusk and darkness they return to mate and lay their eggs. Trout feed on them on all of these occasions.

Mayflies

The mayfly has three stages to its life: nymph, dun and spinner. Nymphs live on stones on the riverbed and drift in the current. They swim to the surface to hatch into a dun. The Dun flies off the water and then moults, returning to the water as a spinner to mate and lay eggs. The spinner dies on laying its eggs and drifts down the river. All these stages are fed on by trout.

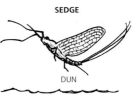

SEDGE

DUN

Mayflies hatch in the middle of the day during the cooler parts of the year and around dawn and dusk in warm weather. Spinners return to the water when it is calm, which is often around dawn and dusk.

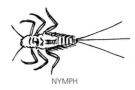

NYMPH

Midges SR SW

Midges are a creature of still or slow moving water, so are found away from the main current in flowing waters. The larvae live in silt so you can expect them to hatch near any silty areas in a river. These larvae are often bright red and are called bloodworms. Although they mainly live in the silt, they also swim around. The pupae swim to the surface to hatch out and are intercepted by trout. The hatches mainly occur around dusk and on into darkness and early in the morning. The adult midge is not as important as a trout food.

MIDGE

57

ADULT

PUPA

Snails SR SW

Snails can be found in great numbers in the slower moving parts of rivers. They are available to trout all of the time, as they live on top of whatever forms the riverbed and in weedbeds.

LARVAE

Terrestrial Insects

When the weather is warm there are a host of insects that are active and get blown onto the water. Terrestrials can make up a large percentage of the food available to trout in less fertile waters, such as high country streams. Brown beetles are usually the first terrestrials to appear in numbers in late spring, followed by green beetles in early and midsummer. Cicadas appear in summer, followed by daddy longlegs in autumn.

Willow grubs drop onto the water throughout the summer, especially on warm days.

Baitfish

Baitfish play a small but significant part in the diet of river trout. Smelt and whitebait are usually present in large numbers when they appear in the tidal reaches of rivers. Trout will gorge on them and put on a lot of weight in a very short time. Late winter and early spring is the time for this feeding frenzy.

Waterboatmen

WATERBOATMAN

This insect lives underwater but breathes air and makes regular trips to the surface to breathe. It has wings and will occasionally fly. Trout intercept it going up to or coming down from the surface, or when it crashes onto the water post flight.

Diving Beetles 🆂🆆

These shiny blackish beetles are about the size of a little fingernail. They breathe air and can fly like a waterboatman. Their larvae too can be found in trout. They look like a caseless caddis and are often mistaken for them. The larvae swim about and are easy pickings.

Dragonflies 🆂🆆

The dragonfly nymph lives in silt on the bed of stillwaters. It hides in the silt and ambushes its prey, but does swim around and it then becomes the prey of trout. The nymphs migrate to shore to hatch and crawl out onto stones or up rushes before breaking out of the nymphal shuck. The adults too are taken by trout when they alight on the water.

Damselflies 🆂🆆

These creatures are closely related to dragonflies and are often erroneously given that name. The nymph, however, is quite different, as it is very active and swims about most of the time. It is long and thin, unlike the thickset dragonfly nymph.

The adult too is different, being smaller and finer than the dragonfly. The main difference is that the adult damselfly folds its wings along its back when it settles, whereas the dragonfly keeps its wings extended at 90 degrees to its body.

Damsel nymphs also crawl out of the water to hatch. There are many more damsels than dragons so they are more commonly found in trout. Trout often jump out of the water to take damselflies as they hover above the water.

DAMSELFLY

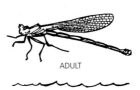

ADULT

LARVAE

59

Where and When to Fish

While most fishers like to see trout rising, trout in most waters can be caught even when they are not rising. Rising times vary from one location to another, and from season to season. Generally speaking dawn and dusk are ideal times to find trout rising on both flowing and stillwaters. In summer fish often rise to insects blown off the land in both types of water. In spring and autumn good rises can be seen during the day on rivers and streams.

Fishing Streams and Rivers

In flowing water we have the choice of casting upstream or downstream. When fishing downstream the fly travels in a series of arcs across the current, covering the water systematically.

If you are a beginner, it is easier to cast downstream because this keeps the line tight. Begin by casting down and across the water at an angle of about 45 degrees, let the fly drift until it is directly below you and retrieve a couple of metres of line before recasting. The fish will often take the fly during this retrieve. Move downstream a metre or so after two or three casts, and keep repeating the process.

Some beginners, as well as some of the experts, make a habit of standing still and covering the same piece of water over and over. This is a waste of time unless you are doing something different every few casts. The fish should take in the first two or three casts if you are using the right fly and covering the water properly, so if you get no response, move on.

You need better control of the line to fish upstream so it is preferable to leave this until you can cast confidently. In upstream fishing the fly is fished in a series of straight lines parallel to the current.

It is worthwhile fishing all the likely places that fish will hide, so try the shadows under trees, in ripples, along undercut banks and weedbeds. Explore the water by casting first up near the bank, first letting the fly drift a few metres back towards you before casting again a few metres further out.

Fishing Stillwaters

Stillwaters come in a range of sizes, from small ponds to very large lakes, and can provide some great fishing. The sheer size of larger stillwaters can be daunting to some, and the lack of features on the water means that it isn't obvious where the fish can be found. Although stillwater trout are continually on the move, certain places are more productive – for example trout often feed around the edges so are not difficult to reach. Always start looking for fish well before you reach the water's edge, so you don't scare from the shallows a fish that could well be caught with just a short cast.

The place where a stream flows into a lake can provide productive fishing. Weedbeds are also a likely place, as fish search for food around

61

their perimeters. Try silty shallows in the early morning or dusk, as they produce good hatches of midge. Trout come in close to feed on terrestrials blown onto the water from tussock or bush, when there is an offshore wind. Waterside rushes are also a likely place when damselflies or dragonflies are hatching, as the nymphs migrate towards them, and use them to crawl out of the water. In hot sunny weather try casting with a terrestrial pattern in the shade of trees or bushes.

Man-made lakes often have old river channels running out from the bank, where trout will cruise in the security of their depths. There is usually ready access to deep water by fishing off the dam, and this can be profitable when the margins are too warm for trout.

Lake outlets are also a good place to fish, if you can find one of the few remaining natural outlets. Unfortunately many have control structures that prevent access.

So think carefully about the best place to fish from, rather than just the easiest.

Stillwaters can be fished blind, the best way being to fish down and across the wind, like fishing downstream in a river. The fly is carried by the drift and you have to retrieve the line slowly. You can cover a lot of water by moving along the shore every few casts.

You can also fish stillwaters to sighted or rising trout, but remember that a rising trout is also on the move, generally up wind. Cast a few metres up wind of where the fish last rose, so that the fly will be seen. You also need to cast well ahead of sighted trout, and this helps to prevent spooking them with the line.

Stillwaters provide a good alternative if rivers are high and temporarily unfishable.

Catch and Release

At this stage you may not be thinking about putting your catch back into the water, but perhaps they may be undersized, and who knows – you may become so proficient that you exceed the bag limit sometime in the future.

Play a trout as quickly as possible. You should remove the hook when the fish is still in the water. If you can't do that, try not to keep the fish out of water for more than 30 seconds. Once you have removed the hook, hold the fish on an even keel in the water, pointing upstream if there is a current, until it swims away of its own accord. It will not survive if you leave it belly up.

Contents

Intelligent Design

"From the far reaches of the universe to the depths of the cell, separate branches of modern science have all discovered astonishing, unexpected fine-tuning – design."

Michael Behe, in 'The Edge of Evolution', Free Press, 2007, p219

An idea whose time has come

S tated simply, 'Intelligent Design' (ID) claims that the natural and living worlds show clear evidence of being designed and are not the result of blind, purposeless forces. Most people who are aware of ID assume, wrongly, that it is a variant of creationism or a form of religious fundamentalism. But when they take time to examine it, many are immediately impressed. In fact, they discover a powerful and self-evident idea. Instinctively, ID feels correct.

But Intelligent Design is not a new idea. For as long as observers of the natural world have wondered how it all came about, there have been those who concluded that the universe is designed. Some ancient Greek philosophers held the view that the world was the result of a creative mind. Intelligent Design in one form or another is, actually, as old as history itself.

Closer to our time, the great architects of modern science like Galileo, Kepler, Newton, Faraday, Kelvin and Pasteur regarded their work in science as exploring the works of an Almighty Creator whose ways were discernible in the natural and living world. And Einstein, whose work on time and space pushed human knowledge to its outer boundaries, acknowledged some kind of mathematical mind

Stated simply, 'Intelligent Design' (ID) claims that the natural and living worlds show clear evidence of being designed and are not the result of blind, purposeless forces.

behind the universe. 'I want to know God's thoughts', he once said, adding, 'the rest are details'.

It is only relatively recently, and largely as a result of the work of Charles Darwin in the nineteenth century, that the idea of an evolving or self-organising universe has gained acceptance. It is now the dominant explanation of origins in the West and an evolutionary framework has become integral to much of Western culture.

In its current form, Intelligent Design poses a formidable challenge to the accepted theories of origins. Drawing on the work of an increasing number of scientists around the world, Intelligent Design questions the current insistence that the origin of life and the universe is a purposeless and undirected process.

ID argues from empirical evidence that is easily detected by scientific enquiry. Its distinguishing characteristic is that it does not appeal to any religious authority, but to scientific investigation alone. This booklet gives a brief overview of that evidence and what distinguishes ID from other explanations of origins.

The cell

Over the last few decades, microbiologists have discovered that each living cell is an unbelievably complex structure. Far from being the simple blob of protoplasm that Darwin envisaged, we now know that its organisation is as complicated as that of a large city with different types of factories, power stations, communication centres, transport systems and storage areas. Every cell is a veritable hive of biochemical activity with carefully differentiated functions controlled by sophisticated information systems. And each one is too small to see with the naked eye!

The human body contains approximately 50 trillion cells. There are over 200 specialised types such as those that make up muscles, tissue, nerves, glands and skin. Each cell is surrounded by a complex membrane which not only protects it from the outside environment but also regulates the transfer of substances in and out of the cell through microscopic pores.

At the core of the cell is the nucleus. It contains almost all the DNA, packed into the chromosomes which carry a complete set of genetic information. The surface of the nucleus has tiny channels through which can pass the information-carrying chemicals which regulate the functions of the cell.

The rest of the cell, the cytoplasm, contains hundreds of different chemicals and a range of tiny bodies or organelles which are responsible for the many

Every cell is a veritable hive of biochemical activity with carefully differentiated functions controlled by sophisticated information systems. And each one is too small to see with the naked eye!

functions of the cell. Among these are the mitochondria which release the energy required by the cell in a controlled chemical reaction. Others store chemicals, release oxygen and dispose of the waste materials of the cell. There is also a complex internal transport system, composed of tiny tubes which act as pathways along which the materials of the cell are moved as required.

Elsewhere within the cell, fats and proteins are synthesised within the reticulum, a labyrinth of active membranes. Located here are the ribosomes which decode the information carried by the messenger RNA from the nucleus about the specific sequences of amino acids required for the production of the full range of proteins. Proteins are fundamental to all the processes of the cell.

In every respect, the cell is a marvel of miniaturization and biochemical engineering.

Norman Nevin, Emeritus Professor of Medical Genetics, Queens University, Belfast, Northern Ireland

The Evidence for Intelligent Design

Design is detectable when there is low probability and high specificity. An object or system can be said to be designed when there is a low probability of it arising by chance or as the result of an existing law or process, and when it matches an existing pattern and fulfils a specific purpose.

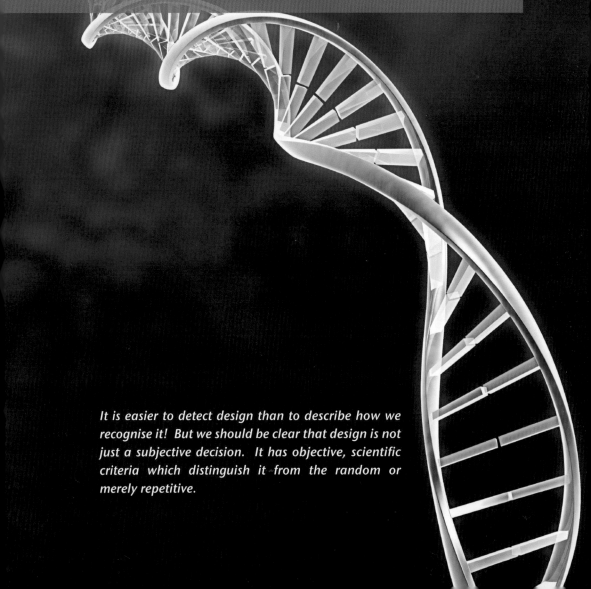

It is easier to detect design than to describe how we recognise it! But we should be clear that design is not just a subjective decision. It has objective, scientific criteria which distinguish it from the random or merely repetitive.

Intelligent Design is based on the observation that natural and living systems show clear evidence of having been designed. To be precise, ID says that 'certain features' of the universe show evidence of design. ID implies that the whole universe is designed, but that the evidence for design is more obvious in some areas than in others. This most certainly does not imply, as some continue to assert, that ID only deals with gaps in our knowledge. Actually, the opposite is true. ID deals, not with what we don't know, but with what we do know.

Intelligent Design is an example of the science of design detection – how to identify patterns arranged by an intelligent cause for a purpose. Design detection is used in a number of scientific fields, such as anthropology, crypto-analysis and the forensic sciences, which seek to explain the cause of events such as a death or fire, and the search for extra-terrestrial intelligence (SETI). The inference that biological information may be the product of an intelligent cause can be tested and evaluated in the same way that scientists test for design in other sciences.

So how and where do we detect design? Let's take the 'how' question first. We know instinctively how to distinguish between designed systems and those that are randomly assembled. We do not ever question whether the thousands of gadgets we use every day are designed – it is obvious that they are. We also recognise collections of things that have been randomly assembled, though the objects in the collection may be individually designed. For example, a rubbish heap is usually a random collection of designed objects.

More importantly, scientists and engineers have identified technical criteria for design. Although these involve fairly complex calculations which draw on information and probability theory, the conclusions are relatively straightforward. Design is detectable when there is low probability and high specificity. This means, essentially, that an object or system can be said to be designed when there is a very low probability of it arising by chance or as the result of an existing law or process, and when it also matches an existing pattern and fulfils a specific purpose.

It is easier to detect design than to describe how we recognise it! But we should be clear that design is not just a subjective decision. It has objective, scientific criteria which distinguishes it from the random or merely repetitive.

Where, then, in natural and living systems can we detect design? Actually it is not difficult. When we apply the criteria for design to natural and living systems, the existence of design is obvious. For example, the universal constants, such as the very precise values of the forces which govern gravity, electricity, magnetism and the various types of chemical and nuclear bonds, appear to be finely tuned to make our planet able to sustain life and suggest intrinsic design. The specified complexity of some living systems, like the eye, the ear or the blood clotting system, is a further clear indicator of design.

But the most compelling argument for design lies in the information content of DNA, the molecule in every living cell which carries much more data than most modern software programmes. We know that information can only arise from prior intelligence and the clear implication of the information content of DNA is that it was assembled by a designing intelligence.

To these matters we now turn in greater detail.

Universal constants

"A common sense approach to the data suggests that a super-intellect has monkeyed with the physics, as well as the chemistry and biology."

Sir Fred Hoyle

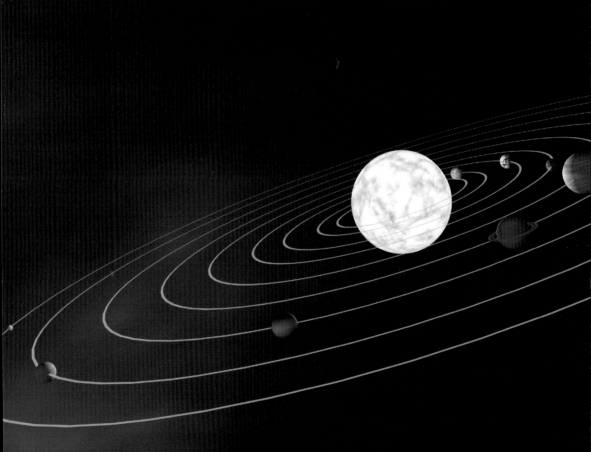

If the moon was not exactly the size it is and in the position it is, the rotation of the Earth would become unstable and life would be unsustainable.

The forces which govern our universe involve a number of physical or mathematical constants whose values must remain within very narrow limits. Such universal constants are involved in determining, for example, the force of gravity, the motion of the planets, the energy of electromagnetic radiation, and the values of the forces that are involved in holding nuclear particles together and those that bond atoms to form molecules.

Taken together, all these forces and their associated physical constants make a varied and impressive set of values which appear to be finely tuned to ensure the maintenance of life on Planet Earth. It has been demonstrated that even tiny variations in these constants and the associated forces they control would make life on earth impossible. For example, if water was a gas at normal temperature, rather than a liquid, as would be predicted purely by the position of its constituent elements in the Periodic Table, life as we know it just could not exist. If the moon was not exactly the size it is and in the position it is, the rotation of the Earth would become unstable and life would be unsustainable.

There are around 20 such universal constants whose values are just right to create the conditions for life as we know it. The probability of arriving at all these values by chance is so incredibly small that it suggests they have been deliberately set.

A common response to this is that we might live in a 'multiverse' with billions of universes, among which ours just happens to have the set of universal constants it does. However, this proposition is highly speculative and incapable of verification. It also deliberately avoids the most obvious explanation, which is what all good scientists consider first until there is good reason to reject it.

Of course the fine tuning of universal constants is not in itself conclusive proof of Intelligent Design. But it is pretty impressive nevertheless and demands a credible explanation. As cosmologist Sir Fred Hoyle has commented, 'A common sense approach to the data suggests that a super-intellect has monkeyed with the physics, as well as the chemistry and biology'.

'Fine tuning' of universal constants

The numerical values that nature has assigned to the fundamental constants, such as the charge on the electron, the mass of the proton, and the Newtonian gravitational constant, may be mysterious, but they are crucially relevant to the structure of the universe that we perceive. As more and more physical systems, from nuclei to galaxies, have become better understood, scientists have begun to realise that many characteristics of these systems are remarkably sensitive to the precise values of the universal constants. Had nature opted for a slightly different set of numbers, the world would be a very different place. Probably we would not be here to see it.

More intriguing still, certain structures, such as solar-type stars, depend for their characteristic features on wildly improbable numerical accidents that combine together fundamental constants from distinct branches of physics. And when one goes on to study cosmology – the overall structure and evolution of the universe – incredulity mounts. Recent discoveries about the primeval cosmos oblige us to accept that the expanding universe has been set up in its motion with a cooperation of astonishing precision.

Paul C W Davies, in 'The Accidental Universe', 1982, Cambridge University Press, preface p vii.

Recent discoveries about the primeval cosmos oblige us to accept that the expanding universe has been set up in its motion with a cooperation of astonishing precision.

Paul Davies

Biological complexity

Modern molecular biology has revealed a cellular world as complex as a galaxy of stars or a modern mega-city. The complexity and variety of the living cell is one of the best kept secrets of the modern world.

The biological research of the last few decades has revealed the remarkable complexity of living things and, in particular, of the living cell. For example, although the 50 trillion (that's fifty thousand billion or 50,000,000,000,000) or so cells which make up the human body are too small to be seen except with a microscope, each one is a veritable nano-technological factory on a grand scale. Far from being the simple blob of protoplasm envisaged by Darwin and his contemporaries, modern biology has revealed a cellular world as complex as a galaxy of stars or a modern mega-city. The complexity and variety of the living cell is one of the best kept secrets of the modern world.

Intuitively, complexity on this scale suggests deliberate design. But there is a more secure basis for that conclusion than intuition. William Dembski, a mathematician and philosopher of science, has studied the complex biochemistry of living systems from the perspective of probability theory. He has demonstrated mathematically that their complexity cannot be explained by chance processes or existing natural laws. He describes the complexity of the cell as 'specified', meaning that it requires the input of specific information to assemble and operate such systems.

A simple analogy clarifies the nature of 'specific complexity'. A safety razor is a useful, and to many people, an indispensable tool. It is clearly designed and, in its own way, complex. The plastic or metal handle is shaped for ease of handling; its head can follow the contours of the skin; and its single or multiple blades protrude to just the right height for effective shaving and to avoid cutting the skin. Although razors come in various shapes, sizes and colours, the basic design is clear. You would never even consider that it was not deliberately designed. It has obviously been constructed according to a previously specified plan.

But what is also clear is that a safety razor is made for a specific purpose. It is not for stripping wallpaper or for removing stains from the carpet. It is specifically designed to remove hair from skin. In that sense it has 'specified complexity' relating to its function. The analogy illustrates that 'specified complexity' relates to both assembly and function.

A further analogy comes from a fax machine. When a fax reaches my office, I do not think that it has been generated by electrical noise, but by someone perhaps many miles away. The message I take out of my machine is not just a random collection of bits of paper and blobs of ink, but an intelligible message. Although the paper I hold in my hand has no physical connection with the paper that was inserted in the fax machine at the sending office, it is 'specified' by the contents of the original document and the information in both originated in the mind of the individual who composed the message. So a fax message which is received in my office has a complexity which is specified by a distant mind and expressed in language which has been transmitted to me.

This indeed is the nature of the complexity found in living systems. For example, the mechanisms in the living cell for producing proteins from amino acids, the essential basis of all life, are colossally complex. They depend on enzymes, which act like chemical ushers which select and modify the individual chemicals which are required in the process. They also involve tiny structures like ribosomes which act like extrusion mechanisms for the

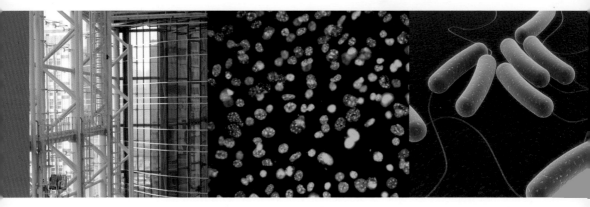

newly formed proteins. The operation of the system for protein synthesis is not only complex, but it is also very specific, generating in different parts of the cell and of the body each one of the thousands of proteins in the exact configurations and quantities required to sustain life. And this is only one example of specified complexity in living systems. There are thousands of them.

Michael Behe, a prominent American biochemist, has taken the idea one stage further. He has concluded that the specified complexity of certain living systems suggest that they are also 'irreducibly complex'. By that he means that each component is required to make the system operate and the removal of any one of them makes it impossible to function.

Many structures we encounter in daily life are irreducibly complex. A mousetrap is a good example of an irreducibly complex system. It has 5 parts and each one is necessary if the device is to catch a mouse. If any one of the parts is removed, the trap will not work.

Behe has used the term to describe the function of the bacterial flagellum, a tail-like structure present in many bacteria. It is, in effect, a biological outboard motor with around 30 parts. It can rotate at speeds of up to 100,000 rpm and has protein parts that act as stators, rotors, O-rings and drive shafts. Behe has noted that the removal of any part of the bacterial flagellum renders it useless. It is, he argues, irreducibly complex.

This points not only to the existence of deliberate design, but also raises a critical problem for accepted evolutionary explanations of its origin. In order to develop a system like the bacterial flagellum, evolutionary theory requires that each intermediate stage, and there would have to be scores of them, has to be fully functional and beneficial to the organism. It is difficult to visualise how a system that requires each one of its 30 parts to be fully operational can gradually evolve by random mutation and natural selection, while maintaining full functionality at each stage, even if the intermediate stages are something other than flagellums.

And again, the bacterial flagellum is only one of hundreds of systems in living things which can be described as irreducibly complex.

Beyond the reach of chance

The Darwinian claim that all the adaptive design of nature has resulted from a random search is one of the most daring claims in the history of science. But it is also one of the least substantiated. No evolutionary biologist has ever produced any quantitative proof that the designs of nature are in fact within the reach of chance. There is not the slightest justification for claiming, as did Richard Dawkins :

> Charles Darwin showed how it is possible for blind physical forces to mimic the effects of conscious design, and, by operating as a cumulative filter of chance variations, to lead eventually to organised and adaptive complexity, to mosquitoes and mammoths, to humans and therefore, indirectly, to books and computers.
>
> **New Scientist,** 15 April, 1982, pp 130-132

Neither Darwin, Dawkins nor any other biologist has ever calculated the probability of a random search finding in the finite time available the sorts of complex systems which are so ubiquitous in nature. Even today we have no way of rigorously estimating the probability or degree of isolation of even one functional protein. It is surely a little premature to claim that random processes could have assembled mosquitoes and elephants when we still have to determine the actual probability of the discovery by chance of one single functional protein molecule!

Michael Denton, Evolution: A Theory in Crisis, Adler and Adler, 1986, p324

DNA, RNA and chromosomes

DNA, or deoxyribonucleic acid, is a remarkable substance. Its molecular structure was first established in the 1950's by James Watson and Francis Crick at Cambridge, who also drew on the earlier work of Maurice Wilkins and Rosalind Franklin in London. Its double helical structure consists of two intertwined sugar-phosphate strands, bonded together by the base pairs adenine (A) which pairs with thymine (T), and cytosine(C) with guanine (G). There are several billion bases in a single molecule of DNA and the genetic information is encoded in the sequences of the bases. RNA (ribonucleic acid) is similar to DNA, but its molecules are shorter and uracil (U) replaces thymine (T). Each triplet of bases codes for an amino acid which is an essential ingredient in the process of protein synthesis.

The information in DNA is held in short sequences or genes, of which there are about 24,500 in the human genome. The DNA is packaged in a highly ordered manner in the chromosomes, of which there are 46 in human cells. Messenger RNA copies segments of the information in DNA and carries it out of the nucleus where it is eventually used to assemble specific proteins in the ribosomes deep within the cell.

The chemical constituents in DNA function like letters in a written language or symbols in a computer code. Just as English letters may convey a particular

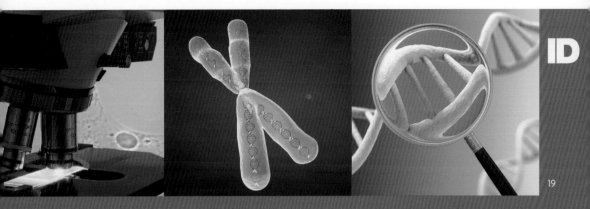

As Richard Dawkins has acknowledged, '**The machine code of the genes is uncannily computer-like.'** Bill Gates has noted, **'DNA is like a computer program, but far, far more advanced than any software we've ever created.'**

message depending on their arrangement, so too do certain sequences of chemical bases along the spine of a DNA molecule convey precise instructions for building proteins. The arrangement of the chemical characters determines the function of the sequence as a whole. Thus, the DNA molecule has the property of 'sequence specificity' that characterises codes and language. As Richard Dawkins has acknowledged, 'The machine code of the genes is uncannily computer-like.' Bill Gates has noted, 'DNA is like a computer program, but far, far more advanced than any software we've ever created.'

After the early 1960s, further discoveries made clear that the digital information in DNA and RNA is only part of a complex information processing system – an advanced form of nanotechnology that both mirrors and exceeds our own in its complexity, design logic and information storage density.

Norman Nevin, Emeritus Professor of Medical Genetics, Queens University, Belfast, Northern Ireland

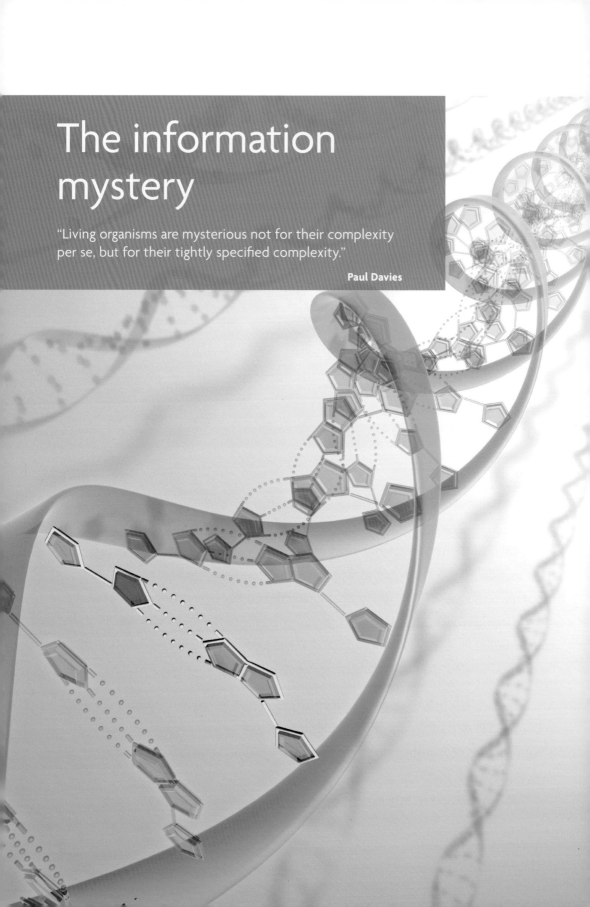

The information mystery

"Living organisms are mysterious not for their complexity per se, but for their tightly specified complexity."

Paul Davies

Paul Davies, in his book 'The Fifth Miracle' (Simon and Schuster, New York, 1999), has identified specified complexity as the key to resolving life's origin. He writes, 'Living organisms are mysterious not for their complexity per se, but for their tightly specified complexity.' He goes on to say that to understand how life arose from inanimate material, we need to know how biologically useful information came to be specified.

Indeed it is the origin of the digitally coded genetic information within the DNA molecule which provides both the enduring mystery of modern biology and the most compelling argument for design in nature. That sort of information carries the potential to generate every living creature which has ever lived and to confer on each one a unique identity. Bill Gates of Microsoft has described the information in DNA as far more complex than any of his software programmes and, of course, he employed software engineers to design them.

Each cell in our bodies contains about 2 metres of DNA. It has been estimated that if we could join up all the DNA in one human body into a single chain, it would reach to the moon and back – 8,000 times! Each molecule of DNA has about 3 billion units of information which is carried in just 4 repeating chemical units or 'base pairs'. But the units do not repeat randomly or repetitively. Each series of three units codes specifically for particular amino acids which are assembled into proteins and ultimately contribute to the unique characteristics of each individual.

Each cell in our bodies contains about 2 metres of DNA. If we could join up all the DNA in one human body into a single chain, it would reach to the moon and back – 8,000 times!

DNA is part of the most sophisticated system of information transfer in the world. It easily outstrips the computerised systems of our age. Occasionally errors arise in DNA transcription, sometimes with devastating consequences for the individual involved. But the extent, precision and durability of the system are truly breath-taking.

Now this poses a fundamental question. Where does this very complex and highly specific information come from? All our experience tells us that information only arises from prior intelligence. The information in a letter comes from the mind of its writer. An article in a newspaper comes from the mind of the journalist who wrote it. The information in a PC comes from the mind of the software engineer who wrote it. There is no known example anywhere of functional information arising randomly or by chance. We only get information from prior intelligence.

So the conclusion about the information content of DNA is obvious. It can only have arisen from a designing intelligence. Of course all scientific conclusions are tentative, but it is not helpful to say that we might someday find an explanation for the origin of information which does not involve intelligence. On this basis, no sensible scientific conclusion could ever be drawn from the data available to us.

The origin of the information in DNA alone is sufficient grounds for proposing the Theory of Intelligent Design.

Information and intelligence

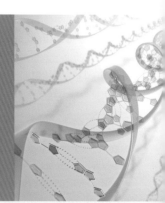

After the early 1960's, further discoveries made clear that the digital information in DNA and RNA is only part of a complex information processing system – an advanced form of nanotechnology that both mirrors and exceeds our own in its complexity, design logic and information storage density.

Where did the digital information in the cell come from? And how did the cell's complex information processing system arise? Today, these questions lie at the heart of origin-of-life research. Clearly the informational features of the cell at least appear designed. And to date, no theory of undirected chemical evolution has explained the origin of digital information needed to build the first living cell. Why? There is simply too much information in the cell to be explained by chance alone. And the information in DNA has also been shown to defy explanation by reference to the laws of chemistry. Saying otherwise would be like saying that a newspaper headline might arise as the result of the chemical attraction between ink and paper. Clearly 'something else' is at work.

Yet, the scientists arguing for Intelligent Design do not do so merely because natural processes, chance, law – or the combination of these – have failed to explain the origin of the information and information-processing systems in cells. Instead, they also argue for design because we know from experience that systems possessing these features invariably arise from intelligent causes. The information on a computer screen can be traced back to a user or programmer. The information in a newspaper ultimately came from a writer – from a mental,

ID

As the pioneering information theorist Henry Quastler observed,
'Information habitually arises from conscious activity.'

rather than a strictly material, cause. As the pioneering information theorist Henry Quastler observed, 'Information habitually arises from conscious activity.'

This connection between information and prior intelligence enables us to detect or infer intelligent activity even from unobservable sources in the distant past. Archaeologists infer ancient scribes from hieroglyphic inscriptions. SETI's search for extraterrestrial intelligence presupposes that information imbedded in electromagnetic signals from space would indicate an intelligent source. As yet, radio astronomers have not found information-bearing signals from distant star systems. But closer to home, molecular biologists have discovered information in the cell, suggesting – by the same logic that underwrites the SETI program and ordinary scientific reasoning about other informational artifacts – an intelligent source for the information in DNA.

DNA functions like a software program. We know from experience that software comes from programmers. We know generally that information – whether inscribed in hieroglyphics, written in a book or encoded in a radio signal – always arises from an intelligent source. So the discovery of information in the DNA molecule provides strong grounds for inferring that intelligence played a role in the origin of DNA, even if we weren't there to observe the system coming into existence.

Dr Stephen Meyer, Director, Discovery Institute, Seattle, in the National Post, Canada, Dec 1st, 2005

Intelligent Design is science

"Even if all the data point to an intelligent designer, such a hypothesis is excluded because it is not naturalistic."

Scott Todd

ID is essentially an interpretation of the data that already exists. There is not much point in gathering more information if you already have enough on which to base your hypothesis.

I t is frequently claimed that ID is not really science and is derived from religious ideas. But the above shows that ID is entirely based on scientific observations and what is sometimes known as 'inference to the best explanation'. The difficulty for some arises because ID proposes an explanation which goes beyond purely material considerations. But that cannot rule it out as science.

Suppose for a moment that a Designing Intelligence actually exists. Are we seriously saying that, if that is the case, science would be unable to recognise it from the material evidence produced by such a Designer? Scott Todd, an eminent American scientist, has actually said as much (Nature, Sept 30th, 1999). He claimed that 'even if all the data point to an intelligent designer, such a hypothesis is excluded because it is not naturalistic'. If that is the case, science is in real trouble. It has all the logic of saying that traffic signals can't exist because some people are colour blind!

It is also claimed that ID is not science because it cannot make predictions that can be tested and that it cannot be falsified by experiment. Assuming that these are criteria for good science – and that is by no means certain – ID is capable of responding positively. As we have seen, there are theoretical criteria for detecting design such as probability and specificity. ID predicts that if you apply these principles to natural and living systems, you will get the answer that design is present. That exercise certainly involves making and testing predictions.

A more recent example comes from the recent and somewhat embarrassing abandonment by the scientific community of the idea of 'junk' DNA. The idea that 90% or more of our DNA is 'junk' because it has no function and represents the accumulated debris of our evolutionary past has been widely promoted. But very recent and convincing data from the study of human DNA indicates that at least 80% of our DNA is active and probably hugely complex. The interesting point here is that ID theorists have been predicting for years that this was likely to be the case within an understanding of biology that includes design. That sounds like a prediction coming true to me.

And on the second point of ID being capable of being falsified, what is necessary is that someone demonstrates that functional information on the scale of DNA can arise without prior intelligence or that there is a clear step-by-step evolutionary pathway with all the intermediary stages to a bacterial flagellum or similar irreducibly complex structure which can be generated by mutations alone. In either case, ID would fail. The fact that no such falsifications are forthcoming, or are likely to be, is testimony to the strength of the design hypothesis.

A further objection to the scientific status of ID is that its theorists do not undertake research and publish in the peer-reviewed literature. In fact, this is quite false. Discovery Institute in Seattle has recently celebrated the publication of the 50th peer reviewed article or paper in the scientific literature, including the work of academics such as Michael Behe, William Dembski, Scott Minnich, Stephen Meyer and Douglas Axe. And further work related to ID is being done in a number of laboratories around the world.

But there are two further points to make about this. In one sense, research work which supports ID is not the central issue. ID is essentially an interpretation of the data that already exists. While gathering more information is useful in confirming a hypothesis, there is already enough on which to base the inference to design. And secondly, when assessing the claim that ID does not publish enough research, it is important to recognise that the peer review process is biased in the direction of the reigning Darwinian paradigm. Papers which argue the ID case are sometimes rejected because they are not judged to be consistent with the accepted naturalistic position on origins. Now there's a real catch 22. You don't publish enough ID research, but we will not approve it anyway because we don't like ID!

Implications

Although ID does not draw on any religious authority, it clearly has philosophical and religious implications. While it does not specify who the Designer is, it provides support for a theistic view of the universe. And it certainly confronts the neo-Darwinian world view that we live in a bleak, purposeless and undirected universe.

Intelligent Design also challenges the view that science can only deal in materialistic explanations – a position known as 'methodological naturalism'. Sean Carroll of California Institute of Technology has given a very clear statement of this position in his 2003 paper now available on the Internet, 'Why (Almost All) Cosmologists are Atheists'. He writes, 'The materialist thesis is simple: that's all there is to the world. Once we figure out the correct formal structure, patterns, boundary conditions and interpretation, we have obtained a complete description of reality'. Revealingly, he then adds in parenthesis, 'Of course we don't have the final answers as to what such a description is, but a materialist believes that such a description does exist'. It is evident that none of that is science. It is, in fact, a philosophical position, a world view, a kind of faith position, posing as a coherent scientific conclusion.

It is becoming increasingly apparent that Darwinism succeeds as a worldview only if it is assumed that there cannot be a non-material explanation of origins. But ID demonstrates that there is clear evidence of intelligent causation of the universe. It is a poor scientist indeed who cannot be sufficiently open-minded to consider the possibility of a non-material origin for the universe, especially when so much of the evidence points in that direction. Science should always go where the evidence leads and should not, as a starting point, rule out one set of explanations.

Intelligent Design is not just good science. It also raises philosophical questions which go to the heart of Western civilisation. It has the potential to make people reflect on the most fundamental questions about their existence. It is, perhaps, because the implications of ID challenge deeply-held beliefs about fundamental questions of life that it is so vehemently opposed without good scientific reasons.

ID and evolution

"Random variation doesn't explain the most basic features of biology. It doesn't explain the elegant sophisticated molecular machinery that undergirds life."

Michael Behe

It is important to say that ID does not dismiss evolutionary processes. ID is about the deep design inherent in the universe whereas evolution is essentially a theory about the processes by which living things develop. They deal, therefore, with quite significantly different aspects of origins.

However, there are two areas in which ID and evolution collide. The first is the implication of neo-Darwinism that life is essentially the result of blind and undirected processes. ID maintains that the science points to deliberate design and discernible intelligence in the natural and living worlds. The second is the claim that random mutation and natural selection can account for the generation of greater genetic complexity over time. ID questions whether there is sufficient evidence that such a mechanism is capable of doing what is claimed.

In any serious discussion of evolution, it is important to know which meaning of 'evolution' is being used. In fact, there are two major and quite different uses of the term 'evolution'.

The first use of the term 'evolution' is what Darwin discovered in the 19th century and essentially refers to the ability of living things to adapt to their environment. Darwin noticed that Nature is able to do what plant and animal breeders have done for centuries. It is clearly possible to breed living things selectively to obtain the particular form that you want. You might want white horses or purple tulips and breeders can select those strains that are most likely to produce the required result.

That Nature can do the same thing is hardly surprising. Natural selection means simply that, by a process of eliminating forms of life which are not suited to a particular environment, living things with specific characteristics survive while the others die. So, for example, birds with short tough beaks will survive if the only available food is nuts with hard shells. Those birds with long slender beaks don't have a chance of surviving. They might, though, if the only available food is soft worms which live 2 inches below the surface of sand. In that case, the birds with the short beaks have no chance of survival.

Birds with short tough beaks will survive if the only available food is nuts with hard shells. Those birds with long slender beaks don't have a chance of surviving. They might, though, if the only available food is soft worms which live 2 inches below the surface of sand.

This form of evolution – sometimes called 'microevolution' – might be better described as 'adaptation'. It really depends on the wide variety of forms of any species which can be produced by the DNA of the species. Natural selection is simply picking out those forms that can best survive in a given environment.

The critical process here is that the wide range of genetic information is significantly narrowed to retain only the desired characteristics. In technical terms we say that the 'gene pool' (ie the total amount of information carried in the DNA of a species) has been reduced by the elimination of those forms of the species which have characteristics which are undesirable.

It is the second use of the term 'evolution' which is much more contentious. In this case it is argued that by a process of random mutation of the information in DNA and natural selection of any beneficial result produced in the form of the living organism, it is possible to increase the complexity of living things. And this is not just a modest claim. The contemporary neo-Darwinian view is that random mutation and natural selection can take us, in an unplanned and undirected process, from a single cell to a human being, via all the other living things in between. This is often referred to as 'macroevolution'.

Such a breathtaking proposition, which is widely and uncritically accepted in Western culture, requires clear proof that there is a mechanism of such creative power. The reality is that the 'mountain' of evidence for evolution is almost entirely about the first type of evolution or adaptation. The evidence for the second version is flimsy in the extreme.

There is a huge inconsistency here. Microevolution necessarily involves an overall reduction in the amount of genetic information. That the evidence for microevolution is used to prove the exact opposite – increasing the complexity of genetic information – is

quite bizarre.

We now know that the genetic information carried in the DNA of every living cell is hugely complex. To suggest that such complexity can be generated by random and undirected processes is a bit like saying that computer software can be generated by letting the wind and rain blow through the laboratories where it is produced. We know that software programmes depend on computer engineers for their design, not on the vagaries of the weather!

Michael Behe, a biochemist and Professor of Biological Science at Lehigh University, Penn, USA, on p83 of his book, 'The Edge of Evolution', puts it like this:

We now know that the genetic information carried in the DNA of every living cell is hugely complex. To suggest that such complexity can be generated by random and undirected processes is a bit like saying that computer software can be generated by letting the wind and rain blow through the laboratories where it is produced.

'But, although Darwin hoped otherwise, random variation doesn't explain the most basic features of biology. It doesn't explain the elegant sophisticated molecular machinery that undergirds life. To account for that – and to account for the root and thick branches of the tree of common descent – multiple coherent genetic mutations are needed. Now that we know what sort of mutations can happen to DNA, and what random changes can produce, we can begin to do the math to find the edge of evolution with some precision. What we'll discover is something quite basic, yet heresy to Darwinists: Most mutations that build the great structures of life must have been non-random.'

Overall, ID claims that, while evolution may contain some of the elements which have produced the variety of living things, it is impossible to conceive of any process for generating the complexity of genetic information which does not involve prior intelligence and design.

And in addition to that we need to find credible explanations for the emergence of life in the first place and also how consciousness exists within our neurobiology. It is overwhelmingly likely that the data will point to design in these areas also.

ID and creationism

The commonest charge levelled against ID is that it is just 'Creationism in a cheap tuxedo'. So what is the connection between the two?

It is important to note that Creationism comes in several forms. Some hold that the earth was created relatively recently – say 10,000 years ago – while others maintain that the creation of the Earth happened billions of years ago. Most creationists hold that the Earth was created progressively in a series of creative acts. For example, the Big Bang, if it actually happened, might have been the original act of creation.

It also needs to be said that creationism, in its central assertion that the universe has a Creator, is a perfectly respectable and reasonable position. Indeed, it is by far the view that has dominated human thought since the beginning of time. It is, to most people who have ever lived, the most credible explanation of why anything is here.

But it is the connection between creationism and science which causes the confusion. Creationism is based, not primarily on scientific observation, though that is part of it, but on religious authority. For example, Christians derive their belief in a Creator ultimately from the teachings of the Bible. Muslims hold the same view on the basis of the teachings of the Koran. Of course, they both find confirmation of their belief in nature and science. But their starting point is essentially religious authority – a valid part of human experience nonetheless.

However, ID is not creationism. ID is derived purely from scientific observations, not from religious authority. Clearly, ID provides support for religious belief, but it does not propose it or depend on it. The criticism that ID is simply another form of Creationism is just simply wrong and arises from a confusion of religious and scientific ideas.

Happy Journal For Women

THINGS
THAT
IGNITE JOY

Discover The Hidden Joys In
Life That Elude You

Krystal Rose